SECURITY & CRYPTOGRAPHY: A HANDBOOK

IN 200 WORDS

KHUSHAL JAIN

Made with ♥ on the Notion Press Platform
www.notionpress.com

To my mother, Smt. Madhu Jain, my father, Sh. Lalit Jain, & my Sister Palak for their constant support, guidance & love (and also for igniting the author in me).

-Khushal Jain

Contents

Contents

Contents

Foreword

Cryptography is an essential component of modern society. It is the science of transforming data in a way that it remains secure even in the presence of adversaries. In today's world, where sensitive information is being transmitted through various communication channels, cryptography has become an indispensable tool to ensure the confidentiality, integrity, and authenticity of this information.

Cryptography has come a long way from its earliest known use in ancient times to its modern-day application in cybersecurity, finance, healthcare, and many other areas. Over the years, cryptography has evolved and diversified, leading to the development of numerous algorithms, protocols, and techniques. Today, cryptography is a vast and complex field, and its applications are continuously expanding.

In this book, you will learn the fundamentals of cryptography, including its history, various encryption techniques, cryptographic algorithms, and applications. You will also explore the challenges associated with cryptography, such as the risks associated with key management and the limitations of various cryptographic techniques.

This book is intended for students, professionals, and anyone interested in understanding the principles and practices of cryptography. It will provide you with a solid foundation to explore the complex world of cryptography and help you appreciate its importance in today's society.

I hope this book will be an informative and engaging read for you!

Preface

When I first started to write this book, I wanted it to be an elaborate text which touches all the topics in detail. While writing, I changed my mind and thought that students suffer the most during the examination time, they know the concepts and they just need insights into the topics. This handbook is also very useful for people willing to start learning cryptography or wants to do something else but some concepts of cryptography are troubling in the way.

I have also tried to sum-up each topic in approximately 200 words so that the readers get a gist of everything.

Although, all these topics are very interesting, worth reading and studying in detail, so do refer to other books and resources to learn in a better and efficient way.

All the content which I have written in this book, I have learnt it all from other books, my teachers, research papers and random sources on internet.

If you think anything is wrong with the concepts or the book content, you can always reach out to me at *khushalj@outlook.com* .

Acknowledgements

I would like to express deep sense of gratitude to my Professor Mr. Abhishek Ankur of Chandigarh University, Mohali for always helping me out with my queries and doubts and always encouraging me to do good.

Special thanks to Professor Namit Chawla, Professor Neha Sharma, Professor Yashika Sharma and Professor Abhinav Raghav of Chandigarh University, Mohali for supporting and encouraging me all the time to do better and for all the programming, networking and security related concepts I know today.
Nothing would have been possible without the support of my teachers.

Lastly, I am indebted to my friends and family members for all the emotional and educational support.

KHUSHAL JAIN

CHAPTER ONE

Cryptography & Its History

Cryptography is the practice of secure communication in the presence of third parties. It is the science of using mathematical techniques to secure communication and protect data. Cryptography has been used throughout history to protect sensitive information and messages. The history of cryptography can be traced back to ancient civilizations such as Egypt and Greece, where they used simple methods of encryption to protect secrets.

As the world evolved, so did cryptography. During World War II, cryptography played a crucial role in the outcome of the war. The Germans used the Enigma machine, a complex encryption device, to transmit secret messages. However, the Allies were able to crack the code, and this gave them a significant advantage.

Today, cryptography is more important than ever. With the growth of the internet and digital communication, the need for secure encryption has become essential. Cryptography is used in many applications such as online banking, e-commerce, and secure communication.

CHAPTER TWO

Monoalphabetic Substitution

A monoalphabetic substitution is a type of encryption technique used to hide a message or information. In this method, each letter of the plaintext message is replaced with another letter or symbol from the same alphabet. For example, the letter "A" could be replaced with the letter "X" in the ciphertext. The substitution is based on a fixed rule or key that is used to encode and decode the message.

Monoalphabetic substitution is a simple method of encryption that can be easily understood and implemented, but it is not very secure. This is because each letter in the plaintext always maps to the same letter or symbol in the ciphertext, making it vulnerable to frequency analysis attacks. In frequency analysis attacks, the attacker analyzes the frequency of the letters in the ciphertext and tries to deduce the corresponding letters in the plaintext.

Therefore, monoalphabetic substitution ciphers are not recommended for sensitive information or messages. More complex encryption methods, such as polyalphabetic substitution ciphers, should be used for better security.

CHAPTER THREE

Single Substitution Cipher

A single substitution cipher is a type of encryption method that replaces each letter of the plaintext message with a unique letter in the ciphertext. This means that the same letter in the plaintext will always be replaced with the same letter in the ciphertext. For example, the letter "A" in the plaintext could be replaced with the letter "X" in the ciphertext, and this substitution will be applied to every occurrence of the letter "A" in the message.

Single substitution ciphers are easy to understand and implement, but they are not very secure. They are vulnerable to frequency analysis attacks, where an attacker analyzes the frequency distribution of letters in the ciphertext to deduce the corresponding letters in the plaintext.

Single substitution ciphers can be improved by using multiple alphabets, known as polyalphabetic substitution ciphers. These ciphers use different substitution rules for different letters or groups of letters in the plaintext, making them more difficult to break. Nonetheless, single substitution ciphers are still useful for simple encryption tasks, such as creating secret codes for games and puzzles.

CHAPTER FOUR

Vigenere Cipher

The Vigenere cipher is a type of encryption technique used to hide a message or information. In this method, each letter of the plaintext message is encoded using a different Caesar cipher based on the letters of a repeating key. The Caesar ciphers are simple monoalphabetic substitution ciphers, where each letter in the plaintext is shifted by a fixed number of positions in the alphabet. The key is used to determine the shift for each letter of the plaintext message.

The Vigenere cipher is more secure than simple monoalphabetic substitution ciphers because it uses multiple alphabets instead of just one. This makes it harder for an attacker to deduce the corresponding letters in the plaintext. However, the Vigenere cipher can still be vulnerable to attacks such as frequency analysis if the key is short or if the plaintext contains repeated patterns.

To make the Vigenere cipher more secure, longer keys can be used, or the key can be randomized. Additionally, modern encryption methods, such as the Advanced Encryption Standard (AES), should be used for sensitive information or messages, as they are much harder to crack.

CHAPTER FIVE

Playfair Cipher

The Playfair cipher is a type of encryption method that is used to hide a message or information. This method was invented by Charles Wheatstone in the 19th century. In this, pairs of letters in the plaintext message are encrypted together. This means that each two-letter pair in the plaintext message is replaced by a different two-letter pair in the ciphertext.

It uses a 5x5 matrix of letters to encode the message. The letters of the alphabet are arranged in the matrix, and the encryption key determines the order of the letters. The encryption key is a word or phrase that is used to generate the matrix. The matrix is created by removing duplicate letters from the encryption key, then adding the remaining letters of the alphabet in order.

It is more secure than other simple encryption methods, such as monoalphabetic substitution ciphers, because it is resistant to frequency analysis attacks. Frequency analysis attacks are used to analyze the frequency of letters in the ciphertext to determine the corresponding letters in the plaintext. It is also resistant to other types of attacks, such as letter-pair analysis and known-plaintext attacks.

However, like any encryption method, the Playfair cipher is not completely secure and can still be broken with enough effort and resources. Nonetheless, it remains a useful tool for encrypting messages and information.

CHAPTER SIX

ADFGVX Cipher

The ADFGVX cipher is a type of encryption technique used to encode and decode messages. It was developed by the German military during World War I and was later used by the French military in World War II. The cipher uses a combination of substitution and transposition techniques to encode messages.

In the ADFGVX cipher, each letter of the plaintext message is first encoded into two different letters, A, D, F, G, V, or X. This is done by using a table that contains these letters in rows and columns. The letter pairs are then transposed using a keyword or phrase to create a new sequence of letters. The resulting ciphertext is a combination of these letters and is much more difficult to decrypt than the original plaintext.

The ADFGVX cipher was considered to be a very secure method of encryption because of its use of multiple steps and the large number of possible combinations. However, it was not perfect and was eventually broken by the Allies during World War II.

Today, the ADFGVX cipher is no longer used for secure communication due to its vulnerabilities. However, it remains an important part of the history of cryptography and has contributed to the development of more advanced encryption techniques

CHAPTER SEVEN

Kerchoff's Principle

Kerchoff's Principle is a principle in cryptography that states that a cryptographic system should be secure even if the attacker knows everything about the system, except for the secret key. This means that the security of a cryptographic system should rely only on the secrecy of the key, and not on the secrecy of the system itself.

In other words, a cryptographic system should be designed in such a way that even if an attacker knows the algorithm used to encrypt the message, the length of the key, and other details about the system, they should not be able to decode the message without knowing the key.

The principle was named after Auguste Kerchoffs, a Dutch linguist and cryptographer who formulated it in the 19th century. Kerchoff's Principle has become a fundamental principle in the design of cryptographic systems and is widely accepted in the field of cryptography.

The importance of Kerchoff's Principle is that it ensures that the security of a cryptographic system does not depend on the secrecy of the system itself, which is difficult to achieve and maintain. Instead, it depends only on the secrecy of the key, which is easier to manage and protect. Therefore, it is recommended to use cryptographic systems that follow Kerchoff's Principle for better security.

CHAPTER EIGHT

Binary Operations

In cryptography, binary operations are used to manipulate and process data in a secure way. Binary operations involve using only two values or digits, usually 0 and 1, to represent data.

One common binary operation used in cryptography is the XOR (Exclusive OR) operation. XOR is a binary operator that takes two inputs, and outputs 1 if exactly one of the inputs is 1, and 0 otherwise. This operation is used in various cryptographic algorithms to produce a ciphertext that is different from the plaintext.

Another important binary operation used in cryptography is the bitwise AND operation. This operation compares the bits of two numbers and outputs a number where the bits are set to 1 only if both corresponding bits in the input numbers are also 1. This operation is used in cryptographic hash functions to generate a unique output that is different for each input message.

Binary operations are also used in cryptographic algorithms such as block ciphers, stream ciphers, and hash functions. These algorithms use a combination of binary operations and other mathematical functions to encrypt data and provide secure communication over the internet and other networks.

In summary, binary operations play an essential role in modern cryptography by providing a reliable and efficient way to process and manipulate data securely.

CHAPTER NINE

Symmetric Key Cryptography

Symmetric key cryptography is a method of encryption where the same key is used for both encryption and decryption of a message or information. This means that both the sender and the receiver share the same key and use it to encode and decode the message.

In symmetric key cryptography, the message is first converted into a coded form or ciphertext using the shared key. The receiver then uses the same key to decrypt the message back into its original form or plaintext. The strength of symmetric key cryptography lies in the secrecy of the shared key, which should be kept private and known only to the sender and receiver.

Symmetric key cryptography is a popular and widely used method of encryption in applications such as online banking, e-commerce, and secure communication. However, one of the main limitations of symmetric key cryptography is the secure distribution of the shared key. If the key is intercepted or obtained by an unauthorized third party, the security of the message is compromised.

To overcome this limitation, more advanced methods of encryption, such as public-key cryptography, have been developed. Public-key cryptography uses two separate keys, one for encryption and one for decryption, which are not shared between the sender and receiver.

CHAPTER TEN

Block Ciphers

Block ciphers are a type of encryption algorithm that operates on fixed-length blocks of data. In this method, the plaintext message is divided into blocks of a fixed length, such as 64 bits. Each block of the plaintext message is then encrypted using a secret key to produce the corresponding ciphertext block.

The key feature of block ciphers is that they are deterministic, meaning that the same plaintext block will always produce the same ciphertext block with the same key. This allows for easy decryption of the ciphertext block using the same key.

Block ciphers are widely used for encrypting large amounts of data, such as in the case of online transactions or secure communication over the internet. They provide a high level of security by using complex mathematical functions and strong keys. However, they are vulnerable to attacks such as brute force attacks, where an attacker tries all possible keys until the correct one is found.

To improve the security of block ciphers, various modes of operation have been developed. These modes define how the plaintext message is divided into blocks and how the blocks are encrypted. Some popular modes of operation include Electronic Codebook (ECB), Cipher Block Chaining (CBC), and Counter (CTR) mode. These modes add an additional layer of security to block ciphers, making them more resistant to attacks.

CHAPTER ELEVEN

Block Cipher Modes

Block cipher modes are methods of encrypting data in blocks of fixed size. There are several block cipher modes, each with its own advantages and disadvantages.

Electronic Codebook (ECB): In this mode, each block of plaintext is encrypted separately using the same key. The advantage of ECB is its simplicity and speed, but it is vulnerable to attacks if the same plaintext blocks are repeated.

Cipher Block Chaining (CBC): In this mode, each block of plaintext is XORed with the previous ciphertext block before encryption. The advantage of CBC is that it is more secure than ECB because each block depends on the previous block, making it more difficult for an attacker to modify the ciphertext.

Cipher Feedback (CFB): In this mode, the ciphertext is fed back into the encryption algorithm to produce the next ciphertext block. The advantage of CFB is that it can be used with stream ciphers, but it is vulnerable to errors in transmission.

Output Feedback (OFB): In this mode, the encryption algorithm is used to generate a keystream, which is then XORed with the plaintext to produce the ciphertext. The advantage of OFB is that it can be used with stream ciphers and is resistant to errors in transmission.

Counter (CTR): In this mode, the encryption algorithm is used to generate a keystream, which is then XORed with a counter to produce the ciphertext. The advantage of CTR is that it can be used with stream ciphers and is resistant to errors in transmission.

The advantages of block cipher modes include their speed, efficiency, and flexibility. They can be used with a wide range of encryption algorithms and are suitable for many different types of applications.

Disadvantages, such as the vulnerability to attacks, the need for secure key management, and the potential for errors in transmission. Therefore, it is important to carefully consider the advantages and disadvantages of each block cipher mode before selecting the best one for a specific application.

CHAPTER TWELVE

Stream Ciphers

Stream ciphers are a type of encryption technique used to secure data in transit. They work by encrypting data one bit at a time, or one byte at a time, as opposed to block ciphers that encrypt a fixed amount of data at a time. In stream ciphers, a secret key is used to generate a sequence of pseudo-random numbers, also known as a keystream. The keystream is then combined with the plaintext data to produce the ciphertext.

Stream ciphers are faster and more efficient than block ciphers, making them ideal for applications that require high-speed encryption and decryption, such as online communication and real-time video streaming. However, they are also less secure than block ciphers because the keystream is generated using a finite key space, which makes them more vulnerable to brute-force attacks.

To overcome this weakness, stream ciphers use techniques such as key whitening, which adds additional randomness to the key to make it more difficult for attackers to predict the keystream. They also use cryptographic protocols such as the Transport Layer Security (TLS) protocol, which provides secure communication over the internet by using a combination of stream ciphers and block ciphers.

Overall, stream ciphers provide a fast and efficient method of encrypting data, but they must be used in conjunction with other cryptographic techniques to ensure secure communication.

CHAPTER THIRTEEN

Fiestal Cipher

The Fiestel cipher is a type of encryption method that is commonly used in computer security to protect sensitive information. It works by taking the plain text that needs to be protected and then putting it through a series of mathematical operations, called rounds, that make it scrambled and unreadable to anyone who doesn't have the key to decrypt it.

The basic idea behind the Fiestel cipher is to divide the plain text into blocks, and then use a key to perform a series of operations on each block. These operations can include things like swapping, shifting, and XOR-ing the bits in the block.

The key is a secret code that only the person who is meant to receive the encrypted message has. Without the key, it is very difficult to unscramble the encrypted message and read the original plain text.

One of the advantages of the Fiestel cipher is that it is very fast and efficient, even when dealing with large amounts of data. It is also relatively easy to implement in software or hardware, which makes it a popular choice for encryption in many applications. However, as with any encryption method, there are ways to break it if the key is not kept secure or if the algorithm is not properly implemented.

CHAPTER FOURTEEN

Unbalanced Fiestal Function

The unbalanced Feistel function is a cryptographic function that is used to encrypt or decrypt data. It is called "unbalanced" because the number of output bits produced by the function is not the same as the number of input bits. This means that the function does not preserve all of the input data in its output.

The unbalanced Feistel function works by dividing the input data into two parts and performing a series of mathematical operations on each part separately. These operations are typically permutations and substitutions that scramble the data in a specific way. Then, the two parts are combined and the process is repeated several times.

The purpose of the unbalanced Feistel function is to provide a high level of security while using a relatively simple algorithm. By applying the same operations repeatedly, the function creates a complex and unpredictable output that is difficult for an attacker to decipher without knowledge of the encryption key.

One important consideration when using the unbalanced Feistel function is the choice of parameters, such as the number of iterations and the specific operations used. These parameters can affect the strength and efficiency of the encryption, so they must be carefully selected based on the specific application and security requirements.

CHAPTER FIFTEEN

DES

DES, short for Data Encryption Standard, is a widely used encryption algorithm designed to protect data and information from unauthorized access. It was developed by IBM in the 1970s and adopted by the US government as an official standard in 1977.

DES uses a symmetric key system, which means that the same key is used for both encryption and decryption. The key size for DES is 56 bits, meaning that there are 2^56 possible keys. This provides a high level of security against brute-force attacks, which attempt to guess the key by trying all possible combinations.

The encryption process in DES involves dividing the plaintext into blocks of 64 bits and applying multiple rounds of permutation and substitution to produce the ciphertext. The ciphertext can be decrypted using the same key and algorithm used for encryption.

Although DES has been widely used for several decades, it is now considered to be insecure due to the key size being too small. Advances in computing technology have made it possible to break the encryption in a reasonable amount of time. As a result, modern encryption methods such as AES (Advanced Encryption Standard) are now used for better security.

CHAPTER SIXTEEN

AES

AES stands for Advanced Encryption Standard. It is a type of encryption algorithm that is widely used to protect sensitive data, such as financial information or personal data, from being accessed by unauthorized users.

Encryption is a process of transforming data into an unreadable format, and AES is an encryption method that uses a series of mathematical operations to transform plain text into cipher text, making it impossible to understand without a key to decrypt it.

AES is a very secure encryption method and has become the standard for protecting data in transit or at rest. It uses a key, which is a long string of numbers, to encrypt and decrypt data. The longer the key, the more secure the encryption.

AES is used in many different applications, such as in email, messaging apps, and online transactions, to protect sensitive data from being intercepted and accessed by unauthorized users. It is also used in hardware devices like USB drives and hard drives to protect the data stored on them.

Overall, AES is an important tool for protecting sensitive information in today's digital world, and its continued development and improvement will play a crucial role in maintaining security for individuals and organizations alike.

CHAPTER SEVENTEEN

Blowfish

Blowfish is a type of encryption algorithm, which is a set of rules for making information secure by scrambling it in a way that can only be understood by someone who has the key to unscramble it. In simple terms, it's like putting a secret code on a message so that only the person with the code can read it.

Blowfish was created by a guy named Bruce Schneier in 1993. It's a fast and efficient algorithm that's widely used to protect sensitive data like passwords, credit card numbers, and other confidential information. Blowfish works by taking a block of data and applying a series of mathematical operations to it to make it difficult to understand.

The strength of Blowfish comes from its key length, which can be as long as 448 bits. This means there are a lot of possible keys that could be used to unscramble the data, making it very difficult for anyone to crack the encryption without the key.

Overall, Blowfish is a reliable and secure encryption algorithm that's stood the test of time. It's used in a wide range of applications, including VPNs, secure email, and secure file storage.

CHAPTER EIGHTEEN

Twofish

Twofish is a type of encryption algorithm used to protect data by scrambling it in a way that only someone with the right "key" can unscramble it. It was developed in the late 1990s as a replacement for the older encryption standard, DES.

The way Twofish works is by taking a block of data and dividing it into smaller pieces, which are then processed in a series of mathematical operations. The key used to encrypt the data is also processed in a similar way, so that the output of the algorithm is different for each unique key.

Twofish is considered a very strong encryption algorithm, as it uses a large key size (up to 256 bits) and a complex set of operations that are difficult to reverse-engineer. This means that it would take a very long time (in the order of millions of years) for an attacker to "brute force" the encryption by trying every possible key combination.

Twofish has been widely adopted for use in various applications, including online banking, secure messaging, and file encryption. It is considered a reliable way to protect sensitive data from unauthorized access.

CHAPTER NINETEEN

IDEA

The IDEA (International Data Encryption Algorithm) is a symmetric key encryption algorithm that is used to protect digital data. Symmetric key encryption algorithms use the same key for both encryption and decryption of data.

The IDEA algorithm uses a block cipher, which means it encrypts data in fixed-size blocks. In the case of IDEA, the block size is 64 bits. The key size for IDEA can vary from 128 bits to 256 bits.

The algorithm works by dividing the data into blocks of 64 bits and then performing a series of mathematical operations on each block using the key. The operations used in IDEA include modular arithmetic, bitwise operations, and table lookups. These operations are repeated for a set number of rounds, with each round modifying the data in a specific way.

The result of the IDEA encryption process is a ciphertext that cannot be read without the key used for encryption. The decryption process is essentially the same as encryption but in reverse, using the same key to undo the modifications made during encryption.

Overall, the IDEA algorithm is widely used in applications that require secure encryption, such as electronic banking, e-commerce, and secure messaging systems.

CHAPTER TWENTY

RC4

RC4, or Rivest Cipher 4, is a symmetric key stream cipher that was designed in 1987 by Ron Rivest. It is widely used in many applications such as secure communication, wireless security, and internet security.

RC4 generates a pseudo-random stream of bytes that is XORed with the plaintext to produce the ciphertext. This stream is generated by a key scheduling algorithm that uses a secret key to initialize the state of the cipher. The key scheduling algorithm operates by swapping elements in a fixed permutation of 256 bytes, based on the secret key.

RC4 has been widely used in many applications due to its simplicity and speed. However, it has been found to be vulnerable to several attacks, such as key recovery attacks and biases in the key stream. Therefore, it is generally not recommended for use in new applications.

In summary, RC4 is a simple and fast stream cipher that has been widely used in many applications for many years. However, due to its vulnerabilities, it is no longer recommended for use in new applications.

CHAPTER TWENTY-ONE

Hash Function

A hash function is a mathematical function that takes in input data of any size and produces a fixed-size output called a hash or digest. The output is typically a unique representation of the input data, meaning that even a small change in the input data will result in a vastly different output.

Hash functions are commonly used in cryptography to verify the integrity of data, such as passwords or digital signatures. When a user creates a password, the hash of that password is stored in a database rather than the password itself. When the user tries to log in, the hash of the password they enter is compared to the stored hash to verify their identity.

Hash functions also have other applications, such as in data structures like hash tables, where they are used to quickly retrieve data based on a key value.

While hash functions have many benefits, such as being quick and easy to use, they also have some limitations. For example, because the output of a hash function is fixed-size, there is always the possibility of two different inputs producing the same output, which is called a hash collision. Additionally, hash functions are one-way, meaning that it is impossible to reverse the process and determine the original input data from the hash output. Finally, hash functions are susceptible to attacks, such as brute-force attacks, where an attacker attempts to guess the input data based on the hash output.

CHAPTER TWENTY-TWO

Hash Salt

A hash salt is a random set of characters that is added to a password before it is hashed. Hashing is a process of converting a password into a unique and fixed-length string of characters, which is more secure than storing the password in plain text.

Adding a hash salt to a password before hashing makes it more difficult for attackers to crack the password. This is because the hash salt adds an extra layer of complexity to the password, making it harder to guess or crack using brute-force attacks.

For example, if a user's password is "password123", a hash salt could be added to create "password123abcd". This new string is then hashed, and the resulting hash value is stored in the database instead of the original password.

When the user logs in, their password is hashed with the same hash salt, and the resulting hash value is compared with the stored hash value. If the two values match, the user is granted access.

In summary, a hash salt is a random set of characters that is added to a password before it is hashed, making it more difficult for attackers to crack the password.

CHAPTER TWENTY-THREE

MD5

MD5 is a type of algorithm used to convert data into a fixed-length, unique string of characters. The algorithm takes in data of any length and produces a 128-bit hash value. The resulting hash value is unique to the input data, meaning that if the input data is changed in any way, the hash value will also change.

MD5 is commonly used for data integrity checks to ensure that data has not been tampered with or corrupted during transmission or storage. It is also used for password encryption to ensure that the password cannot be easily reversed to its original form.

While MD5 was widely used in the past, it has been found to have security weaknesses and is no longer recommended for use in new applications. Attackers can manipulate the input data in such a way that the resulting hash value will be the same as the original data, making it possible to tamper with the data without being detected.

Therefore, it is recommended to use more secure hashing algorithms, such as SHA-256 or SHA-3, which are more resistant to attacks and provide stronger security.

CHAPTER TWENTY-FOUR

MD6

MD6 is a cryptographic hash function, which means it takes a message of any length and produces a fixed-size output, called a hash value. The hash value is used to verify the integrity of the message, meaning any changes to the message will result in a different hash value.

MD6 was developed by Ronald Rivest, who is also the creator of several other hash functions like MD5 and SHA-1. MD6 is an improved version of MD5, with better security features and improved performance.

MD6 uses a compression function that combines the input message with a chaining value and other parameters to produce an intermediate hash value. The compression function is applied repeatedly to process the message in blocks until a final hash value is produced.

MD6 has several security features, including resistance to collision attacks, length extension attacks, and birthday attacks. It also supports variable-length hash values and has a built-in mechanism to prevent multi-collision attacks.

In summary, MD6 is a secure and efficient cryptographic hash function that can be used for a wide range of applications, including message authentication, digital signatures, and password storage.

CHAPTER TWENTY-FIVE

SHA & Its Types

SHA, or Secure Hash Algorithm, is a type of cryptographic algorithm that is used to generate a fixed-length output from any given input data. This output is often referred to as a "hash", and it serves as a digital fingerprint of the input data.

There are several types of SHA algorithms, including SHA-1, SHA-2, and SHA-3. Each type of SHA algorithm has its own unique characteristics and is used for different purposes.

SHA-1 is the oldest and most widely used SHA algorithm. It generates a 160-bit hash and is commonly used for digital signatures and other forms of authentication.

SHA-2 is a family of SHA algorithms that includes SHA-224, SHA-256, SHA-384, and SHA-512. These algorithms are more secure than SHA-1 and generate longer hashes, ranging from 224 to 512 bits. They are commonly used in applications that require higher levels of security, such as online banking and e-commerce.

SHA-3 is the newest addition to the SHA family and was designed to provide an alternative to SHA-2. It generates hashes of various lengths, including 224, 256, 384, and 512 bits, and is designed to be more secure and efficient than SHA-2.

In summary, SHA algorithms are important tools in cryptography and are used to ensure the security and integrity of digital information. Each type of SHA algorithm has its own strengths and weaknesses, and choosing the right one depends on the specific needs of the application.

CHAPTER TWENTY-SIX

RIPEMD

RIPEMD is a family of cryptographic hash functions that are used to secure and authenticate data. Hash functions take data of any length and turn it into a fixed-length string of characters, which is called a hash. This hash can be used to verify that the original data has not been tampered with, and to ensure that the data has not been corrupted during transmission.

RIPEMD was created as a more secure alternative to the MD4 and MD5 hash functions, which were found to have weaknesses that made them vulnerable to attacks. The RIPEMD family of hash functions includes RIPEMD-128, RIPEMD-160, RIPEMD-256, and RIPEMD-320. These different versions provide varying levels of security, with longer hash values generally considered to be more secure.

RIPEMD uses a complex algorithm to create its hash values, which makes it difficult for attackers to reverse-engineer the original data from the hash. This helps to protect sensitive information, such as passwords, credit card numbers, and personal identification data.

RIPEMD is widely used in a variety of applications, including secure messaging, digital signatures, and secure communication protocols. Its security and reliability have made it a popular choice for many organizations that need to protect their data from cyber threats.

CHAPTER TWENTY-SEVEN

MAC

> *"DO NOT CONFUSE WITH THE MAC YOU STUDY IN COMPUTER NETWORKS FOR PHYSICAL ADDRESS. THAT IS MEDIA ACCESS CONTROL ADDRESS AND THIS IS MESSAGE AUTHENTICATION CODE."*

A Message Authentication Code, or MAC for short, is a way to ensure that a message has not been tampered with or modified during transmission.

Imagine you want to send a message to someone, but you're worried that someone else might intercept it and change the contents of the message. A MAC can help prevent this by generating a code or "tag" that can be attached to the message. This tag is based on the contents of the message and a secret key that only you and the intended recipient know.

When the recipient receives the message, they can use the same key and the contents of the message to generate their own tag. If the tag they generate matches the one you sent, they can be sure that the message has not been tampered with. If the tags do not match, then the message may have been modified, and the recipient should not trust its contents.

MACs are often used in computer networks and other communication systems to ensure that messages are authentic and have not been tampered with. They provide an extra layer of security that can help prevent unauthorized access and protect the integrity of the data being transmitted.

CHAPTER TWENTY-EIGHT

HMAC

HMAC stands for Hash-based Message Authentication Code. It's a way to make sure that a message hasn't been tampered with during transmission.

Here's how it works: first, you take the message that you want to send, and you "hash" it. A hash is like a digital fingerprint - it's a unique string of characters that represent your message.

Next, you take a secret key (a password or code) that only you and the recipient know, and you use that to "sign" the message. Basically, you take the hashed message and the secret key, and you combine them in a specific way to create a unique code that only you and the recipient can create.

When the recipient gets the message, they can run the same process with the secret key and the message they received. If the resulting code matches the one you sent, they know that the message hasn't been changed or tampered with during transmission.

Overall, HMAC is a simple but effective way to add an extra layer of security to your messages. By using a secret key and a hash, you can make sure that your messages are protected against tampering or unauthorized access.

CHAPTER TWENTY-NINE

Asymmetric Key Cryptography

Asymmetric key cryptography is a method of encrypting and decrypting messages using two different keys: a public key and a private key. The public key is used for encrypting messages, while the private key is used for decrypting them.

The two keys are mathematically related, but it's impossible to figure out the private key just by knowing the public key. This means that you can share your public key with anyone without worrying about someone intercepting your messages, as they won't be able to decrypt them without your private key.

Here's an example: Let's say Alice wants to send a message to Bob. Bob generates a pair of keys: a public key and a private key. He shares his public key with Alice. Alice uses Bob's public key to encrypt the message, and sends it to him. Bob uses his private key to decrypt the message and read it.

This method is called asymmetric key cryptography because the two keys are different. It's also sometimes called public key cryptography, because the public key can be shared publicly. Asymmetric key cryptography is used in many secure communication systems, such as HTTPS, SSH, and PGP.

CHAPTER THIRTY

Euler's Toient

The Euler Totient function, also known as Euler's Totient or Euler's Phi function, is a mathematical function that is used to calculate the number of positive integers that are relatively prime to a given positive integer.

To understand this function, we need to first understand what it means for two numbers to be relatively prime. Two numbers are said to be relatively prime if they do not have any common factors other than 1. For example, 6 and 35 are relatively prime because their only common factor is 1.

The Euler Totient function takes a positive integer n as input and returns the number of positive integers less than or equal to n that are relatively prime to n. For example, the value of the Euler Totient function for the number 8 is 4, because there are 4 positive integers less than or equal to 8 that are relatively prime to 8 (i.e., 1, 3, 5, and 7).

The Euler Totient function has many applications in number theory and cryptography. It is used, for example, in the RSA encryption algorithm, which is used to secure online transactions and protect sensitive information.

CHAPTER THIRTY-ONE

Modular Arithmetic

Modular arithmetic is a way of doing math that is different from what you may have learned in school. Instead of working with regular numbers, modular arithmetic works with remainders. When you divide a number by another number, the remainder is the number that is left over.

In modular arithmetic, we only work with remainders that are less than a given number called the modulus. For example, if we're working with modulo 7, then we only use remainders between 0 and 6.

The basic operations of addition, subtraction, and multiplication work the same way as regular arithmetic, but with one key difference: after each operation, we take the remainder of the result when divided by the modulus.

For example, let's say we're working with modulo 7. If we add 3 and 5, we get 8. But in modular arithmetic, we only care about the remainder when dividing by 7, which is 1. So, $3 + 5 \equiv 1 \pmod{7}$. The symbol "≡" means "is congruent to".

Modular arithmetic has many applications in computer science, cryptography, and number theory. It is used to solve problems related to cycles, repetition, and patterns.

CHAPTER THIRTY-TWO

Fibonacci Numbers

Fibonacci numbers are a sequence of numbers that start with 0 and 1, and each subsequent number is the sum of the previous two numbers. So, the sequence goes like this: 0, 1, 1, 2, 3, 5, 8, 13, 21, 34, 55, and so on. These numbers are named after an Italian mathematician named Fibonacci, who introduced the sequence to Western mathematics in the 13th century.

Fibonacci numbers are fascinating because they occur naturally in many things in the world around us. For example, the number of petals on a flower, the spirals on a pinecone or a seashell, and the growth patterns of certain plants all follow Fibonacci sequences.

These numbers also have many interesting properties and applications in mathematics and other fields. For instance, they appear in number theory, algebra, geometry, and even in music and art.

Fibonacci numbers have captured the imagination of mathematicians and non-mathematicians alike for centuries, and they continue to be studied and appreciated today.

CHAPTER THIRTY-THREE

Birthday Theorem

The Birthday Theorem is a mathematical concept that helps us understand the likelihood of two people sharing the same birthday in a group of people. It states that in a group of 23 people, there is a more than 50% chance that at least two people share the same birthday.

This might seem surprising at first, but it's actually quite logical. There are 365 days in a year (excluding leap years), and each person in the group can have a birthday on any one of those days. As the group size increases, the number of possible pairs of people with matching birthdays increases rapidly, making it more and more likely that at least one such pair exists.

The Birthday Theorem has many real-world applications, from understanding the likelihood of a data breach to analyzing voting patterns. But remember, while the theorem gives us a good idea of the probability of two people sharing a birthday, it's not a guarantee!

CHAPTER THIRTY-FOUR

Birthday Paradox

The Birthday Paradox is a fascinating mathematical concept that shows how the probability of two people sharing the same birthday increases as more people are added to a group.

At first, it might seem unlikely that two people in a group of, say, 23, would share the same birthday. But when you start to calculate the probability, you'll be surprised.

The probability of two people in a group of 23 sharing the same birthday is actually around 50%. That means that if you gather 23 people in a room, it's more likely than not that at least two of them will share the same birthday!

This paradox happens because there are only 365 possible birthdays in a year (not including leap years), but as more people are added to a group, the number of possible birthday pairs increases rapidly. The more people you add, the more likely it becomes that at least two of them will share a birthday.

The Birthday Paradox has many practical applications, from cryptography to risk management. It also serves as a great example of how probability can be surprising.

CHAPTER THIRTY-FIVE

Birthday Attack

A birthday attack is a type of cryptographic attack that exploits the mathematical principle called the birthday paradox. The birthday paradox states that in a group of randomly chosen people, there is a high probability that two people will have the same birthday, even though there are 365 possible birthdays.

In a birthday attack, an attacker tries to find a collision, which is when two different inputs produce the same output. For example, in a hash function, the attacker tries to find two different messages that produce the same hash value.

The attack works by generating a large number of random inputs and computing their hash values. As the number of inputs increases, the probability of finding a collision also increases, eventually reaching a point where it becomes almost certain.

Birthday attacks are particularly dangerous because they can compromise the security of cryptographic systems that rely on hash functions, such as digital signatures or message authentication codes. To protect against birthday attacks, cryptographic systems use hash functions with a larger output size, which reduces the likelihood of collisions.

CHAPTER THIRTY-SIX

Random Number Generator

A random number generator (RNG) is a computer program or device that produces numbers that appear to be chosen at random. It's like rolling a dice or picking a number out of a hat, except the computer is doing it for you.

RNGs are used in many applications, including video games, cryptography, simulations, and scientific experiments. They're also used in gambling, where the randomness of the numbers is important to ensure fairness.

There are two types of RNGs: true random number generators (TRNGs) and pseudo-random number generators (PRNGs). TRNGs use physical processes, such as radioactive decay or thermal noise, to generate truly random numbers. PRNGs, on the other hand, use algorithms to generate numbers that appear random but are actually determined by a set of rules.

PRNGs are more common than TRNGs because they're faster and easier to implement. However, they're not truly random and can be predicted if the algorithm and seed (starting value) used to generate the numbers are known.

In summary, an RNG is a tool that produces random-seeming numbers, and it's useful in many applications. But it's important to understand the type of RNG being used and its limitations when it comes to true randomness.

CHAPTER THIRTY-SEVEN

NAOR-Reinhold

NAOR-Reinhold is a cryptographic algorithm used to create a shared secret between two parties without actually sharing any secret information. This process is called key agreement.

The algorithm works by having each party choose a secret number and perform some mathematical operations with a publicly known value. These operations create a shared value that both parties can use as a secret key to encrypt and decrypt messages.

The security of the NAOR-Reinhold algorithm relies on the difficulty of solving certain mathematical problems. Even if an eavesdropper intercepts the publicly transmitted information, they should not be able to determine the secret key without solving these problems, which is computationally difficult.

The NAOR-Reinhold algorithm is widely used in internet security protocols, such as SSL/TLS and SSH, to establish secure connections between clients and servers. This helps ensure that sensitive information, such as passwords and financial transactions, are transmitted securely and cannot be intercepted or read by unauthorized parties.

Overall, NAOR-Reinhold is a valuable tool for creating secure communication channels, and its use in internet security protocols helps ensure that sensitive information is protected.

CHAPTER THIRTY-EIGHT

Mersenne Twister Pseudorandom Function

A pseudorandom function is a way to generate numbers that appear random but are actually created by an algorithm. The Mersenne Twister is one such pseudorandom function that is commonly used in computer programming.

The Mersenne Twister works by starting with a seed value, which is a number that the algorithm uses to generate the first random number. From there, it creates a sequence of numbers that appear to be random, but are actually deterministic - meaning that given the same seed value, the same sequence of numbers will always be produced.

One advantage of the Mersenne Twister is that it produces high-quality random numbers. This means that the numbers it generates are statistically similar to true random numbers, meaning that they are not biased towards any particular value or pattern.

The Mersenne Twister is also relatively fast and efficient, making it well-suited for use in computer programs and applications that require random number generation. However, it is important to note that because the Mersenne Twister is a deterministic algorithm, it should not be used for cryptographic purposes where true randomness is required.

CHAPTER THIRTY-NINE

Linear Congruential Generator

A Linear Congruential Generator (LCG) is a type of algorithm used to generate random numbers. The way it works is by taking a starting number, called the seed, and then applying a set of mathematical operations to it to generate a new number. This new number becomes the seed for the next calculation, and the process repeats itself over and over again.

The formula for an LCG typically looks like this:

$X_{n+1} = (aX_n + c) \bmod m$

In this formula, X_n is the current seed, X_{n+1} is the next seed, a and c are constants, and m is the modulus. The modulus is the maximum value that the generated number can have.

LCGs are often used in computer programs that require random numbers because they are fast and easy to implement. However, they are not considered to be the most secure method of generating random numbers, as their output can be predicted if an attacker knows the seed and the constants used in the formula.

In summary, an LCG is a simple algorithm that generates a sequence of random numbers by using a starting value and applying a set of mathematical operations to it. While it is fast and easy to use, it is not the most secure method of generating random numbers.

CHAPTER FORTY

Blum Blum Shub

Blum Blum Shub (BBS) is a pseudorandom number generator algorithm that is commonly used in cryptography to generate random numbers. The algorithm was invented by Lenore Blum, Manuel Blum, and Michael Shub in 1986.

The basic idea behind BBS is to generate a long sequence of random bits by repeatedly squaring a large number and taking the middle bits of the result. The starting number is chosen to be the product of two large prime numbers, which makes it difficult to predict the sequence of bits that will be generated.

To generate a random number using BBS, the algorithm needs a starting value, which is usually a large prime number. This starting value is then squared and the middle bits of the result are taken as the first random number. The result is then squared again to generate the second random number, and so on.

The security of BBS relies on the difficulty of factoring the starting number, which is a large composite number made up of two prime numbers. If an attacker can factor this number, they can predict the sequence of random numbers that will be generated by the algorithm.

BBS is a simple and efficient algorithm that can generate long sequences of random bits. It is widely used in cryptography for tasks such as key generation, encryption, and digital signatures.

CHAPTER FORTY-ONE

Diffie Hellman

Diffie-Hellman is a key exchange algorithm that allows two parties to securely communicate with each other even if they have never met before. The algorithm was invented by Whitfield Diffie and Martin Hellman in the 1970s and is widely used in modern cryptography.

The Diffie-Hellman algorithm works by allowing two parties, usually called Alice and Bob, to agree on a shared secret key without actually sharing the key itself. Instead, they exchange some public information that can be used to derive the key.

To do this, Alice and Bob each choose a secret number and perform some mathematical operations on these numbers to generate a public value that they send to each other. Using the public values they received, they can perform additional mathematical operations to derive the same shared secret key.

The security of the Diffie-Hellman algorithm comes from the fact that it is difficult to derive the secret key from the public values exchanged between Alice and Bob. As long as the secret numbers chosen by Alice and Bob are kept secret, the shared key will be secure.

Overall, the Diffie-Hellman algorithm is a simple and elegant way for two parties to establish a shared secret key without having to transmit the key itself over an insecure communication channel.

CHAPTER FORTY-TWO

RSA

RSA is an encryption technique used to keep information safe when it is being transmitted over a network or stored on a device. It was invented by Ron Rivest, Adi Shamir, and Leonard Adleman in 1977, and is named after their initials.

The technique uses two keys: a public key and a private key. The public key can be shared with anyone, while the private key is kept secret. When someone wants to send a message to someone else, they use the recipient's public key to encrypt the message. Once the message is encrypted, only the recipient's private key can be used to decrypt it. This means that only the intended recipient can read the message, even if it is intercepted by someone else during transmission.

The RSA encryption technique is based on the fact that it is very difficult to factor large numbers. The public and private keys are generated using large prime numbers and complex mathematical calculations. The security of RSA is based on the fact that it would take an impractical amount of time for a computer to factor the large numbers used to generate the keys.

Overall, RSA is a widely used encryption technique that helps to keep sensitive information safe from unauthorized access.

CHAPTER FORTY-THREE

Digital Signature

A digital signature is an electronic method of verifying the authenticity and integrity of a digital document or message. It's like a virtual fingerprint that identifies the sender of a message and ensures that the contents of the message have not been altered in any way during transmission.

Digital signatures are based on complex mathematical algorithms that generate unique codes, called hash values, which are used to verify the identity of the sender and the integrity of the message. The sender's private key is used to create a digital signature, while the recipient uses the sender's public key to verify the signature.

Digital signatures are commonly used to sign important documents like contracts, agreements, and legal papers, as well as to ensure the security and integrity of online transactions like online banking and e-commerce. They provide a level of security and authenticity that traditional signatures can't match, as they can be easily forged or tampered with.

In summary, a digital signature is a secure and reliable way to confirm the authenticity and integrity of digital documents and messages, ensuring that they have not been altered or tampered with during transmission.

CHAPTER FORTY-FOUR

Elliptic Curve Cryptography

Elliptic Curve Cryptography (ECC) is a type of cryptography that is used to secure communications and transactions. It uses a mathematical concept called elliptic curves to create public and private keys that are used to encrypt and decrypt messages.

In ECC, a user generates a private key that is kept secret, and a corresponding public key that is shared with others. The public key is used to encrypt messages, and the private key is used to decrypt them. The security of ECC comes from the fact that it is difficult to calculate the private key from the public key.

ECC is often used in applications where resources are limited, such as on mobile devices or in Internet of Things (IoT) devices. This is because ECC requires less processing power and memory compared to other encryption methods like RSA.

ECC is also used in various protocols like HTTPS, SSL/TLS, and SSH to secure internet communications. It is considered to be a strong encryption method and is widely used in the industry to secure sensitive data.

Overall, ECC is a powerful tool for securing data and communications, and its use is becoming increasingly widespread in the modern digital landscape.

CHAPTER FORTY-FIVE

ElGamal Encryption

ElGamal encryption is a type of public-key encryption that allows two people to communicate securely over an insecure channel. The two people involved are usually referred to as the sender and the receiver.

The sender uses the receiver's public key to encrypt the message before sending it over the insecure channel. Once the receiver receives the encrypted message, they use their private key to decrypt it and read the original message.

The ElGamal encryption scheme uses a mathematical concept called a discrete logarithm problem to ensure the security of the encryption. This means that even if an attacker intercepts the encrypted message, they would not be able to decrypt it without the private key.

One advantage of ElGamal encryption over other public-key encryption schemes is that it allows for "perfect forward secrecy." This means that even if an attacker manages to obtain the private key at a later time, they would not be able to decrypt past messages that were encrypted using the public key.

Overall, ElGamal encryption provides a secure and reliable way for two parties to communicate over an insecure channel without compromising the confidentiality of their messages.

CHAPTER FORTY-SIX

Digital Signature Scheme

A digital signature scheme is a way of verifying the authenticity and integrity of electronic documents, messages or data. It involves the use of cryptographic algorithms and keys to create a unique digital signature that can be used to prove the identity of the signer and ensure that the contents of the document have not been tampered with.

The process of creating a digital signature involves using a private key to encrypt a hash of the document being signed. The resulting encrypted value is the digital signature, which can be verified by anyone using the corresponding public key. If the signature matches the document, then the document has not been altered since it was signed, and the signer can be verified.

Digital signature schemes provide several benefits, including:

Authentication: The signature proves that the document was created by a particular person or entity.

Integrity: The signature ensures that the contents of the document have not been altered since it was signed.

Non-repudiation: The signer cannot later deny having signed the document, as their signature is unique to them.

Digital signature schemes are widely used in e-commerce, online contracts, and other electronic transactions to ensure security and trust.

CHAPTER FORTY-SEVEN

Public Key Infrasture

Public Key Infrastructure (PKI) is a system that allows secure communication over the internet by using digital certificates and public key cryptography. In simple terms, it's a way to ensure that the information you're sending and receiving online is protected from being intercepted or altered by unauthorized parties.

PKI works by using two keys, one public and one private. The public key is used to encrypt data, while the private key is used to decrypt it. These keys are stored in digital certificates, which are issued by trusted third-party organizations called Certificate Authorities (CAs).

When you send a message, your computer encrypts it using the recipient's public key. Only the recipient, who possesses the corresponding private key, can decrypt the message. This ensures that no one else can read the message, even if they intercept it.

PKI also provides a way to verify the identity of the person or organization you're communicating with online. Digital certificates issued by CAs include information about the certificate holder, such as their name and website URL. By verifying this information, you can be sure that you're communicating with the intended recipient and not a malicious impostor.

In summary, PKI is a system that uses digital certificates and public key cryptography to provide secure communication and verify the identity of online entities.

CHAPTER FORTY-EIGHT

Digital Certificate

A digital certificate is a type of electronic identification that is used to verify the identity of someone or something online. It contains information such as the name of the owner, their email address, and the name of the organization that issued the certificate.

Think of it like a digital passport that proves who you are online. Just like how a passport has your picture, name, and other important information, a digital certificate has your identity information, but in a digital format.

Digital certificates are used to secure online transactions, such as online banking, online shopping, and accessing secure websites. They are issued by a trusted third-party, known as a certificate authority (CA), which verifies the identity of the owner of the certificate.

When you visit a website that has a digital certificate, your web browser checks the certificate to make sure it is valid and issued by a trusted CA. If the certificate is valid, your web browser will establish a secure, encrypted connection to the website to protect your information from being intercepted by hackers.

Overall, digital certificates play a crucial role in online security by verifying the identity of online entities and enabling secure online transactions.

CHAPTER FORTY-NINE

X.509

X.509 is a standard format for encoding digital certificates that are used in public key cryptography. These certificates are used to verify the authenticity of a person or organization's identity, and to ensure that communications between two parties are secure and private.

In simple terms, a digital certificate is like a digital ID card that proves the identity of its owner. It contains information such as the owner's name, public key, and the name of the organization that issued the certificate. X.509 is a standard way of formatting this information so that it can be read and understood by different computer systems.

The X.509 format is based on a hierarchical structure, where certificates are issued by Certificate Authorities (CAs) who are trusted to verify the identity of the certificate owner. This creates a chain of trust, where each certificate in the chain is verified by the previous certificate in the chain.

X.509 certificates are commonly used in a variety of applications, such as web browsing, email, and virtual private networks (VPNs). They are an essential component of modern digital security and help ensure that online communications are secure and reliable.

The X.509 format structure is made up of a set of fields that contain information about the digital certificate. These fields include the version number, the serial number, the issuer name, the subject name, the public key, and the validity period.

The version number field specifies the version of the X.509 standard that the certificate adheres to. The serial number field is a unique identifier for the certificate. The issuer name field contains the name of the organization that issued the certificate. The subject name field contains the name of the entity that the certificate represents.

The public key field contains the public key that is used to encrypt and decrypt messages between the certificate holder and other parties. The validity period field specifies the date and time range during which the certificate is considered valid.

The X.509 format structure is used to ensure that digital certificates are standardized and can be easily understood by different systems and applications. It is an important part of online security and helps to establish trust between parties in online transactions.

CHAPTER FIFTY

Kerberos

Kerberos is a system used for secure authentication, which means verifying the identity of a user or a system. It was developed at MIT and is widely used in computer networks, especially in corporate environments.

Working: When a user logs into a system, their username and password are sent to the Kerberos authentication server. The server generates a ticket-granting ticket (TGT), which is sent back to the user's computer. The TGT is then used to request service tickets for specific services, like accessing a file server or email account. The service tickets are encrypted and can only be read by the user's computer and the service they are trying to access.

One of the benefits of Kerberos is that it uses a "trusted third party" approach to authentication. This means that the user's password is never sent over the network, which reduces the risk of it being intercepted by an attacker. Additionally, because the service tickets are encrypted, even if an attacker were to intercept them, they would not be able to read the information inside.

Overall, Kerberos is an important tool for ensuring secure authentication in computer networks, and it helps keep sensitive information safe.

CHAPTER FIFTY-ONE

Pretty Good Privacy

PGP is a computer program that provides encryption and decryption of electronic messages and files. Encryption is the process of encoding a message in such a way that only authorized parties can read it, while decryption is the process of decoding the encrypted message back into its original form. PGP uses a combination of symmetric and asymmetric encryption methods to secure data.

PGP was created by Phil Zimmermann in 1991 to protect the privacy of email communication. It quickly gained popularity as a tool for secure communication, especially among activists, journalists, and whistleblowers who need to communicate sensitive information without the risk of it being intercepted or read by unauthorized parties.

PGP works by creating a unique key pair for each user. The first key is a public key, which is freely distributed to anyone who wants to communicate with the user. The second key is a private key, which is kept secret by the user and is used to decrypt messages that are encrypted with their public key. This means that only the intended recipient can decrypt the message, as they are the only one who has access to the private key.

PGP has become an industry standard for secure communication, and its principles have been integrated into many other encryption tools and protocols. It remains an essential tool for protecting sensitive information, and its importance continues to grow in today's world of digital communication.

CHAPTER FIFTY-TWO

Steganography

Steganography is a technique of hiding secret information within an innocent-looking image, audio or video file in a way that makes it difficult for others to detect. It is a way of sending secret messages without anyone else knowing about it.

The process involves taking the secret message or data and embedding it into another file, such as an image or audio file. The information can be hidden in various ways such as changing the color of specific pixels in an image or altering the audio frequencies in a song. The secret message can only be retrieved by someone who knows how to decode it using a specific algorithm or method.

Steganography is often used for covert communication purposes, such as sending secret messages between spies, terrorists or other covert groups. It is also used for data protection, as sensitive information can be hidden in plain sight and transported without drawing attention. However, it can also be used for malicious purposes, such as to conceal malware or illegal content.

Overall, steganography is a powerful tool that allows for the transmission of secret information, but it should be used responsibly and ethically.

CHAPTER FIFTY-THREE

Types of Steganography

Image Steganography: This type of steganography involves embedding secret data within images. The hidden information is typically embedded within the least significant bits of the image pixels. This method is relatively easy to implement and difficult to detect.

Audio Steganography: Audio steganography is similar to image steganography, but the secret data is embedded within audio files. The hidden data can be encoded within the frequency spectrum of the audio file or within the least significant bits of the audio samples.

Video Steganography: This type of steganography involves hiding secret information within video files. The information can be hidden within the least significant bits of the video frames or within the frequency spectrum of the video.

Text Steganography: Text steganography involves hiding secret information within text documents. The hidden data can be encoded within the white spaces, punctuation marks, or within the letter casing.

Network Steganography: Network steganography involves hiding secret data within network traffic. The information can be embedded within the protocol headers, payloads, or within the timing of the network packets.

CHAPTER FIFTY-FOUR

Steganography V/S Cryptography

Steganography and cryptography are two different techniques used to protect information.

Cryptography involves converting a message into an unreadable form that can only be understood by someone who has the decryption key. This means that anyone who intercepts the message cannot understand its contents without the key. Cryptography is like putting a message in a locked box: only those who have the key can open it.

Steganography, on the other hand, involves hiding a message within another seemingly innocent message, such as a picture or audio file. The hidden message is often encrypted to further increase its security. This means that even if someone intercepts the message, they will not even know that there is a hidden message within it. Steganography is like hiding a secret message within a larger message, hoping that no one notices it.

In summary, cryptography makes the message unreadable to anyone who does not have the key, while steganography hides the message within another message to make it harder to detect. Both techniques can be used together for even greater security.

CHAPTER FIFTY-FIVE

Steganalysis

Steganalysis is the process of detecting hidden messages or information within digital files such as images, audio or video files, that have been concealed using a technique called steganography.

Steganography involves embedding a secret message within a larger file, such as an image, by making small modifications to the file that are difficult to detect. For example, a message may be hidden by slightly altering the colors of certain pixels in an image, or by changing the spacing between words in a block of text.

Steganalysis is the process of trying to detect these hidden messages by analyzing the files for any irregularities or patterns that may indicate the presence of a hidden message. This can involve looking for changes in the file size, color distribution, or other aspects of the file that may be different from what would be expected from a normal file.

Steganalysis is important for a variety of reasons, including detecting and preventing illegal activities such as terrorism or espionage, as well as ensuring the integrity of digital files in fields such as forensics or data storage. By detecting hidden messages, steganalysis helps to protect digital security and ensure that files are used in a responsible and ethical manner.

CHAPTER FIFTY-SIX

Cryptanalysis

Cryptanalysis is the study of secret codes, also known as cryptography, and the techniques used to break them. The goal of cryptanalysis is to uncover the hidden message within a code without having the key or secret that was used to create it.

To do this, cryptanalysts use a variety of methods, including frequency analysis, which looks at how often certain letters or patterns of letters appear in the code, and brute-force attacks, which involve trying every possible key until the correct one is found.

Cryptanalysis can be used for both good and bad purposes. Governments and intelligence agencies may use cryptanalysis to decode secret messages sent by other countries or organizations. Criminals, on the other hand, may use it to break into computer systems or steal sensitive information.

The development of cryptanalysis has led to advancements in cryptography as well. As cryptanalysts find new ways to break codes, cryptographers must create stronger and more secure methods to protect information.

In summary, cryptanalysis is the study of secret codes and the methods used to break them. It can be used for both good and bad purposes and has led to advancements in the field of cryptography.

CHAPTER FIFTY-SEVEN

Night Before Exams

If you haven't studied much and you have an exam tomorrow, you can refer to these cheat sheets for a summary of everything.

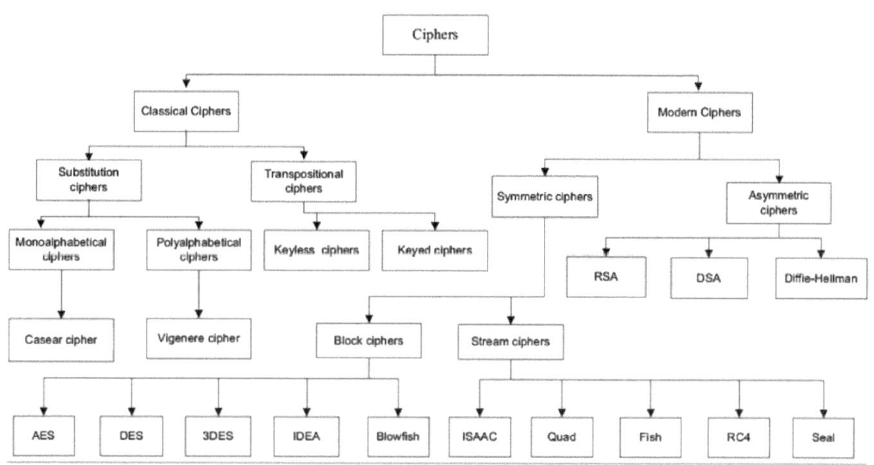

Classification of Ciphers

Symmetric – Performance	
Algorithm	**Cipher Type**
Hieroglyphics – First Known Cipher	None
Scytale (400 BC by the Spartans)	Transposition
Caesar	Mono-Substitution
Vigenere	Poly-Substitution
Vernam (One Time Pad) – Used in WWII in the German Enigma	XOR
DES [Lucifer] (56 bits)	Block
3DES (2 keys – 112 bits & 3 keys - 168 bits)	Block
AES [Rijndael] (128, 192, 256 bits)	Block
Blowfish	Block
Twofish	Block
IDEA	Block
RC2	Block
RC4 (used by WEP and WPA)	Stream
RC5	Block
RC6	Block
CAST	Block
MARS	Block
Serpent	Block
Twofish	Block
E0 (used by BlueTooth)	Stream

Symmetric Cryptography Cheat Sheet

Asymmetric (Public Key Crypto) – Key Exchange
Diffie-Hellman Key Exchange (DH)
Digital Signature Algorithm (DSA)
El Gamal Encryption Algorithm
Elliptic Curve Cryptography (ECC)
Rivest, Shamir & Aldeman Encryption Algorithm (RSA)
Knapsack - *Defunct*

Asymmetric Cryptography Cheat Sheet

Key Management and Certificate Lifecycle
Key Generation – a public key pair is created and held by the CA
Identity Submission – The requesting entity submits its identity to the CA
Registration – the CA registers the request and verifies the submission identity
Certification - The CA creates a certificate signed by its own digital certificate
Distribution – The CA publishes the generated certificate
Usage – The receiving entity is authorized to use the certificate only for its intended use
Revocation and expiration – The certificate will expire or may be revoked earlier if needed
Renewal – If needed, a new key pair can be generated and the cert renewed
Recovery – possible if a vertifying key is compromised but the holder is still valid and trusted
Archive – certificates and users are stored

Authentication
Kerberos – ticket based system, symmetric key KDC
CHAP – exchange of hashed values
Certificates used w/I a PKI for Asymmetric key
Username & **Password** most common
Token-based auth requires possession of token
Biometric authentication

Certificates
X.509 – User's public key, the CA (Certificate Authority) distinguished name, and the type of symmetric algorithm used for encryption.

SSL
The Secure Sockets Layer Protocol has two parts. **First**, the **SSL Handshake Protocol** establishes the secure channel. **Next**, the **SSL Application Data Protocol** is used to exchange data over the channel. 6 Steps in the handshaking process.

ISAKMP
(Internet Security Association and Key Management Protocol) used to negotiate and provide authenticated keying material for security associations in a protected manner
Authentication of peers Threat management Security association creation and management Cryptographic key establishment and management

Bell La-Padula access control model
SOAS subjects objects access modes security levels

Diffie-Hellman algorithm
a secret key exchange over an insecure medium without any prior secrets.

Cheat Sheet

Symmetric Block Style Algorithms			
Name	Rounds	Keysize	Blocksize
Lucifer	16	128	128
DES	16	64 (56)	64
3DES	48	128 (112) 192 (168)	64
Blowfish	16	32-448 128-default	64
Twofish	16	128,192,256	128
IDEA	8	128	64
CAST-128	16	40-128	64
CAST-256	48	128,160,192,-224,256	128
RC2	18	0-1024	64
RC5	0-255	0-2048	32,64,128
RC6	20	128,192,256	128
AES	10,12,14	128,192,256	128
SAFER SK64	8-10	64,128	64,128
SAFER SK128	8,12,16	128,192,256	128
Mars	32	128-448	128
Skipjack	32	80	64
Serpent	32	128,192,256	128
Seed	16	128	128
Misty1	any multiple of 4	128	64
Gost	32	256	64
Clefia	18,22,26	128,192,256	128
Camellia	18,24	128,192,256	128
ARIA	12,14,16	128,192,256	128
TEA	16,32	128	64
ICE	16	64	64
SHACAL-1	80	128-512	160
SHACAL-2	80	128-512	256

Symmetric Block Algorithms

Symmetric Streaming Algorithms	
Name	Keysize
RC4	40-2048
W7	128
Sober	128
Rabbit	128
SEAL	160

DES Block Modes
ECB – Electronic Code Book
CBC – Cipher Block Chaining
CFB – Cipher Feedback
OFB – Output Feedback
CTR – Counter Mode

AES Methods
SubBytes
ShiftRows
MixColumns
AddRoundKey

Symmetric Algorithms

Asymmetric Encryption

Uses publicprivate key pair

Each user generates a pair of public and private keys

Public Key is known to everyone and is used to encrypt data

Private Key is only known to the key owner and used for decryption

Used in 3 categories

-Encryption/Decryption (provide secrecy)

-Digital signatures (provide authentication)

-Key exchange (of session keys)

Diffie-Hellman key exchange

First public-key type scheme

Proposed by Diffie & Hellman in 1976

A practical method for public exchange of a secret key

Cannot be used to exchange an arbitrary message

Security relies on the difficulty of computing discrete logarithms

Diffie-Hellman algorithm

q	prime number
α	α<q ,α primitive root of q
User A	
Select PR=Xa	Xa<q
Calculate PU=Ya	Ya=α^Xa mod q
User B	
Select PR=Xb	Xb<q
Calculate PU=Yb	Yb=α^Xb mod q
Secret key calculation	
User A	K=(Yb)^Xa mod q
User B	K=(Ya)^Xb mod q

Disadvantages

Cannot be used for asymmetric key exchanges

Man-in-the-Attack

ElGammal-Cryptosystem

Presented in 1984 by Tather Elgammal

Used for encrypting messages

Based on discrete lagarithmic problem

Disadvantages

Decryption is slow

Duplicates message length by factor of two during encryption

ElGammal algorithm

Select large prime	q
Select	p , p is primitive root of q
User A	
Choose private key	Xa , 1 < Xa < q-1
Compute public key	Ya=p^Xa mod q
Similarly User B calculates Xb and Yb	
Encryption from A	
Message M	0<=M<=q-1
Choose k	1<=k<=q-1
Compute	K=Ya^k mod q
Compute	C1=p^k mod q
Compute	C2=KM mod q
---Ciphertext(C1,C2)	
Decryption from B	
Recover key	K=C1^Xa mod q
Compute message	M=C2*K-1 mod q

RSA

Uses large integers (eg.1024 bits)

RSA key generation

Select two large primes p and q	p not equal to q
Calculate	n<--p*q
Calculate	O(n)<--(p-1)*(q-1)
Select e	1<e<O(n) and e is coprime to O(n)
Calculate	d<--e^-1mod O(n)
Public key	PU={e,n}
Private key	PR={d,n}
Encryption	
Plaintext	M<n
Ciphertext	C=M^e(mod n)
Decryption	
Plaintext	C
Ciphertext	M=C^d(mod n)

Key Distribution Techniques

Means of delivering key to two parties who wish to communicate

For symmetric encryption to work,two parties must exchange the same key

Public-key cryptosystems are mostly used to encrypt secret keys

Frequent key exchanges are desirable to limit the amount of data compromised

The strength of any cryptographic system relys on key distribution technique

Advantages and Disadvantages

Hard to crack since it involves factorization of prime numbers

Can be very slow in cases where large data needs to be encrypted

Man-in-the-Middle attack

Cheat Sheet

Key Distribution Models

Model 1

A->B PUa||IDa

B->A E(PUa,ks)

-Ensures confidentiality but not authentication

-Vulnerable to man-in-the-middle attack

Model 2

A->B E(PUb,[N1||IDa])

B->A E(PUa,[N1||N2])

A->B E(PUa,N2)

A->B E(PUb,E(PRa,Ks))

-ensures both confidentiality and authentication

Distribution of public keys:

Public announcement

Feeding in a Publicly available directory

-Both vulnerable to forgery(anyone can claim to be someone)

Public Key Authority

-A trusted third party(KDC)

-Provides session keys to users who wish to communicate

-Requires users to be registered

-Just like a directory composed of users public key

-User interacts with the directory to obtain any desired public key securely

Interaction Model:

A->auth Request|T1

auth->A Epr_auth[KPU_b|Request|T1]

A->B Epu_b[IDA|N1]

B->auth Request|T2

auth->B Epr_auth[KPU_a|Request|T2]

B->A Epu_a[N1|N2]

A->B Epu_b[N2]

Public-Key Certificates:

Certificates allow key exchange without realtime access to Public-Key Authority

A certificate binds user identity to public key

Certificate contains all necessary details appended by its hash

Helps user claim accountability for a Key

X_509 Certificates:

Issued by a Certification Authority (CA)

Part of CCITT X.500 directory service standards

Defines the framework for authentication

Uses public-key crypto & digital signatures

X.509 certificates are widely used and has 3 versions

Each version with information extended

Certificate contains information such as Public Key, Digital Signature, Issuer, Version, Serial Number, Time Stamp.

X.509 Version 3:

Has been recognised that additional information is needed in a certificate

-email/URL, policy details, constraints

Rather than explicitly naming new fields defined a general extension model

-Identifier, Criticality Indicator, Value

Hash Functions

Accepts variable length input M and produces fixed-size hash h

h = H(M)

Principal object is data integrity

It is infeasible to find object

- With pre-specified hash **(One-Way Property)**

-Two objects mapping to same hash**(Collision -Free Property)**

Message Authentication Code(MAC):

Also known as a keyed hash function

Concerned with integrity and authentication

Calculates hash from the message and encrypts with the secret key->Cryptographic Checksum or MAC or Tag

-Then is appended to the message

-The reciever calcutates the hash of message and compares

-Same hash value confirms that the message came from the stated sender (its authenticity) and has not been changed.

Digital Signatures :

Concerned with integrity, authentication, Non-repudiation

Operation is similar to that of the MAC

Model-1:

Instead the hash value of a message is encrypted with a user's private key

Anyone who knows the user's public key can verify the integrity of the message

An attacker who wishes to alter the message would need to know the user's private key

-This provides authentication.

Model 2 :

Once the encrypted hash of the message is calulated and appended to original message

Once again it is encrypted with the symmetric secret key

Reciever decrypts it with the symmetric key then public key

Then calculates hash of message and compares

This ensures confidentiality as well as authentication

Cheat Sheet

Caesar Cipher
$C = (M + k) \bmod n$
$M = (C - k) \bmod n$

Multiplicative Cipher
$C = (M * k) \bmod n$
$M = (C * k\text{-}1) \bmod n$

Affine Cipher
$C = [(M * k1) + k2] \bmod n$
$M = [(C - k2) * k1\text{-}1] \bmod n$

Vigenere Cipher
The plaintext(P) and key(K) are added modulo 26.
$Ei = (Pi + Ki) \bmod 26$

Decryption:
$Di = (Ei - Ki + 26) \bmod 26$

	1	2	3	4	5
1	A	B	C	D	E
2	F	G	H	I,J	K
3	L	M	N	O	P
4	Q	R	S	T	U
5	V	W	X	Y	Z

Polybius Square

Input: bus
Output: 124543

	A	B	C	D	E	F	G	H	I	J	K	L	M	N	O	P	Q	R	S	T	U	V	W	X	Y	Z
A	A	B	C	D	E	F	G	H	I	J	K	L	M	N	O	P	Q	R	S	T	U	V	W	X	Y	Z
B	B	C	D	E	F	G	H	I	J	K	L	M	N	O	P	Q	R	S	T	U	V	W	X	Y	Z	A
C	C	D	E	F	G	H	I	J	K	L	M	N	O	P	Q	R	S	T	U	V	W	X	Y	Z	A	B
D	D	E	F	G	H	I	J	K	L	M	N	O	P	Q	R	S	T	U	V	W	X	Y	Z	A	B	C
E	E	F	G	H	I	J	K	L	M	N	O	P	Q	R	S	T	U	V	W	X	Y	Z	A	B	C	D
F	F	G	H	I	J	K	L	M	N	O	P	Q	R	S	T	U	V	W	X	Y	Z	A	B	C	D	E
G	G	H	I	J	K	L	M	N	O	P	Q	R	S	T	U	V	W	X	Y	Z	A	B	C	D	E	F
H	H	I	J	K	L	M	N	O	P	Q	R	S	T	U	V	W	X	Y	Z	A	B	C	D	E	F	G
I	I	J	K	L	M	N	O	P	Q	R	S	T	U	V	W	X	Y	Z	A	B	C	D	E	F	G	H
J	J	K	L	M	N	O	P	Q	R	S	T	U	V	W	X	Y	Z	A	B	C	D	E	F	G	H	I
K	K	L	M	N	O	P	Q	R	S	T	U	V	W	X	Y	Z	A	B	C	D	E	F	G	H	I	J
L	L	M	N	O	P	Q	R	S	T	U	V	W	X	Y	Z	A	B	C	D	E	F	G	H	I	J	K
M	M	N	O	P	Q	R	S	T	U	V	W	X	Y	Z	A	B	C	D	E	F	G	H	I	J	K	L
N	N	O	P	Q	R	S	T	U	V	W	X	Y	Z	A	B	C	D	E	F	G	H	I	J	K	L	M
O	O	P	Q	R	S	T	U	V	W	X	Y	Z	A	B	C	D	E	F	G	H	I	J	K	L	M	N
P	P	Q	R	S	T	U	V	W	X	Y	Z	A	B	C	D	E	F	G	H	I	J	K	L	M	N	O
Q	Q	R	S	T	U	V	W	X	Y	Z	A	B	C	D	E	F	G	H	I	J	K	L	M	N	O	P
R	R	S	T	U	V	W	X	Y	Z	A	B	C	D	E	F	G	H	I	J	K	L	M	N	O	P	Q
S	S	T	U	V	W	X	Y	Z	A	B	C	D	E	F	G	H	I	J	K	L	M	N	O	P	Q	R
T	T	U	V	W	X	Y	Z	A	B	C	D	E	F	G	H	I	J	K	L	M	N	O	P	Q	R	S
U	U	V	W	X	Y	Z	A	B	C	D	E	F	G	H	I	J	K	L	M	N	O	P	Q	R	S	T
V	V	W	X	Y	Z	A	B	C	D	E	F	G	H	I	J	K	L	M	N	O	P	Q	R	S	T	U
W	W	X	Y	Z	A	B	C	D	E	F	G	H	I	J	K	L	M	N	O	P	Q	R	S	T	U	V
X	X	Y	Z	A	B	C	D	E	F	G	H	I	J	K	L	M	N	O	P	Q	R	S	T	U	V	W
Y	Y	Z	A	B	C	D	E	F	G	H	I	J	K	L	M	N	O	P	Q	R	S	T	U	V	W	X
Z	Z	A	B	C	D	E	F	G	H	I	J	K	L	M	N	O	P	Q	R	S	T	U	V	W	X	Y

Vigenere Table

Cheat Sheet

Ending

For issues and removal of any content you can contact me at khushalj@outlook.com

9 798889 864752

Printed by Libri Plureos GmbH in Hamburg,
Germany